SEASONS

SEASONS

An Illustrated Treasury

Compiled by Michelle Lovric

COURAGE BOOKS

an imprint of
RUNNING PRESS
Philadelphia, Pennsylvania

Royle

Copyright © 1993 by Royle Publications Limited
Royle House
Wenlock Road
London N1 7ST
England
Concept developed by Michelle Lovric
53 Shelton Street
Covent Garden
London WC2H 9HE
England

Canadian representatives: General Publishing Co., Ltd., 30 Lesmill Road, Don Mills, Ontario M3B 2T6.

9 8 7 6 5 4 3 2 1
Digit on the right indicates the number of this printing.

Library of Congress Cataloging-in-Publication Number 93–070583
ISBN 1–56138–326--0
Cover design by Toby Schmidt
Cover illustration after Miles Birket Foster
Interior design by Robert Perry
Text edited by Melissa Stein
Typography by Deborah Lugar

Published by Courage Books, an imprint of Running Press Book Publishers
125 South Twenty-second Street
Philadelphia, Pennsylvania 19103

The author gratefully acknowledges the permission of the following to reproduce copyrighted material in this book:

p. 16: From *Earth Weather as Explained by Professor Xargle* by Jeanne Willis. Copyright © 1992 by Jeanne Willis. Used by permission of Dutton Children's Books, a division of Penguin Books USA Inc.

p. 37: From "The Last Flower of Autumn" by Edith Södergran, from *Edith Södergran: Complete Poems*, translated by David McDuff, published by Bloodaxe Books in 1984.

NATURE PAINTS THE WORLD ACCORDING TO ITS SEASONS. THE LIVING POETRY OF THE EARTH IS COMPOSED OF SUCCEEDING STANZAS OF BUDS, LEAVES, FLOWERS, AND FRUIT, INSPIRING THE POET TO REACH FOR A PEN, AND THE PAINTER FOR A PALETTE.

EACH SEASON BRINGS ITS OWN PAGEANT AS PART OF THE ENDLESS CYCLE OF RENEWAL. SPRING CONSOLES AND INVIGORATES AFTER THE CHILL OF WINTER — THE YELLOWS OF ITS BLOSSOMS PROMISE THE STRONGER WARMTH TO COME. ITS GENTLE RAINS MAKE OUR PROSPECTS GREENER. SUMMER LENGTHENS THE DAY AND FILLS THE LANDSCAPE WITH DENSE FOLIAGE, BREATHING CERTAINTY INTO THE WAVERING WARMTH OF SPRING. AUTUMN, GENTLE AND REFLECTIVE, SOOTHES THE BLAZE AND FLARE OF SUMMER WITH ITS DIM, MISTY SILHOUETTES. WINTER BRINGS A BRACING COLD, STRIPPING NATURE TO ITS BARE SOUL, SHROUDING THE LAND IN THE PURITY OF SNOW.

NATURE'S OWN BOUNDLESS CREATIVITY SPARKS THE IMAGINATIONS OF ARTISTS AND WRITERS. THIS BOOK, UNITING WORDS AND IMAGES OF THE SEASONS, EXPRESSES THE SEASONS' GIFTS TO THE SENSES AND TO THE SPIRIT.

All that is harmony for you, my
Universe, is in harmony with me as
well. Nothing that comes at the
right time for you is too early or
too late for me. Everything is fruit
to me that your seasons bring,
Nature.

MARCUS AURELIUS ANTONINUS (121–180 A.D.)
ROMAN EMPEROR

To him who in the love of nature holds

Communion with her visible forms, she speaks

A various language; for his gayer hours

She has a voice of gladness, and a smile

And eloquence of beauty, and she glides

Into his darker musings, with a mild

And healing sympathy . . .

William Cullen Bryant (1794–1878)
American poet

IT IS ALWAYS SUNRISE
SOMEWHERE; THE DEW IS
NEVER ALL DRIED AT ONCE; A
SHOWER IS FOREVER FALLING;
VAPOR IS FOREVER RISING.

John Muir (1838–1914)
Scottish-born American naturalist

The earth goes on, clothes herself at every dawn with fresh beauty, and rejoices to herself. Our dark hearts cast no shadow over her, and our heavy foot-steps are not felt.

Gertrude Bell
(1868–1926)
British writer

The day is an epitome of the year.
The night is the winter, the morning
and the evening are the spring and
fall, and the noon is the summer.

HENRY DAVID THOREAU (1817–1862)
AMERICAN WRITER

RENEW THYSELF COMPLETELY EACH DAY; DO IT AGAIN, AND AGAIN, AND FOREVER AGAIN.

CONFUCIUS [KUNG CHTU] (551-479 B.C.), CHINESE PHILOSOPHER

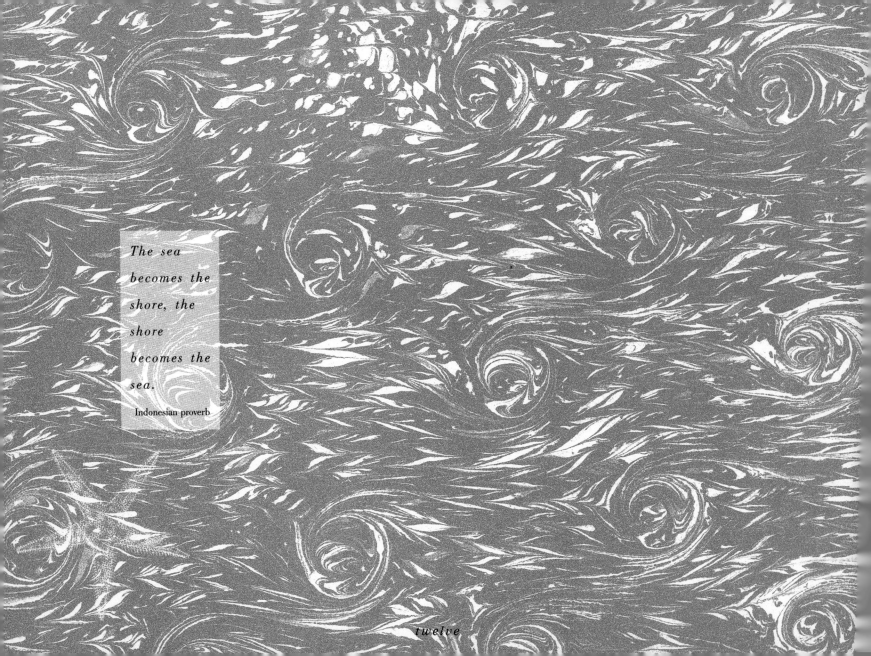

> *The sea
> becomes the
> shore, the
> shore
> becomes the
> sea.*
>
> Indonesian proverb

... THE EVENING MIST CLOTHES
THE RIVERSIDE WITH POETRY, AS
WITH A VEIL, AND THE POOR
BUILDINGS LOSE THEMSELVES IN
THE DIM SKY, AND THE TALL
CHIMNEYS BECOME CAMPANILI,
AND THE WAREHOUSES ARE
PALACES IN THE NIGHT, AND THE
WHOLE CITY HANGS IN HEAVENS,
AND FAIRY-LAND IS BEFORE US—
....NATURE, WHO, FOR ONCE,
HAS SUNG IN TUNE, SINGS HER
EXQUISITE SONG TO THE
ARTIST...

James McNeill Whistler (1834–1903)
American painter

$\mathcal{L}$iving Nature, not dull Art

Shall plan my ways and rule my heart.

JOHN HENRY CARDINAL NEWMAN (1801–1890)
ENGLISH PRELATE AND THEOLOGIAN

LET US GIVE NATURE A CHANCE; SHE KNOWS HER BUSINESS BETTER THAN WE DO.

Michel Eyquem de Montaigne (1533–1592)
French writer

THERE ARE FOUR SORTS
[OF WEATHER].
TOO HOT.
TOO COLD.
TOO WET AND TOO WINDY.

Jeanne Willis, b. 1957
English writer

[The twelve months]

Snowy, Flowy, Blowy,

Showery, Flowery, Bowery,

Hoppy, Croppy, Droppy,

Breezy, Sneezy, Freezy.

George Ellis (1753–1815)
The Twelve Months

Simple and fresh and fair from winter's close emerging,
As if no artifice of fashion, business, politics, had ever been,
Forth from its sunny nook of shelter'd grass—
  innocent, golden, calm as dawn,
The Spring's first dandelion shows its trustful face.

Walt Whitman (1819–1892)
American poet

Spring has
returned.
The earth
is like a
child
that knows
poems.

RAINER MARIA RILKE (1875-1926)
CZECH-BORN GERMAN POET

When the hounds of Spring are on winter's traces,

The mother of months in meadow or plain

Fills the shadows and windy places

with lisp of leaves and ripple of rain.

Algernon Swinburne (1837–1909)
English poet

. . . Spring unlocks the flowers to

paint the laughing soil. . .

REGINALD HEBER (1783–1826)
ENGLISH BISHOP AND HYMN-WRITER

My beloved spake, and said unto me, Rise up, my love, my fair one, and come away. For, lo, the winter is past, the rain is over and gone; the flowers appear on the earth; the time of the singing of birds is come, and the voice of the turtle is heard in our land; the fig tree putteth forth her green figs, and the vines with the tender grape give a good smell. Arise, my love, my fair one, and come away.

THE SONG OF SOLOMON
VERSE 2: 10–13

Ah, the bird-like fluting

Through the ash-tops yonder

Bullfinch-bubblings, soft sound suiting

What sweet thoughts, I wonder?

Robert Browning (1812–1889)
English poet

THE SPRING IS GONE—LIGHT, GENIAL-HEARTED SPRING!

WHOSE BREATH GIVES ODOR TO THE VIOLET,

CRIMSONS THE WILD ROSE, TINTS THE BLACKBIRD'S WING,

UNFOLDS THE BUTTERCUP. SPRING THAT HAS SET

TO MUSIC THE LAUGHTER OF THE RIVULET,

SENT WARM PULSATIONS THROUGH THE HEARTS OF HILLS,

RECLOTHED THE FORESTS, MADE THE VALLEYS WET

WITH PEARLY DEW . . .

Charles Sangster (1822–1893)
Canadian poet

Nature, like man, sometimes weeps for gladness.

BENJAMIN DISRAELI (1804–1881)
ENGLISH PRIME MINISTER

For me kind Nature wakes her genial pow'r,

Suckles each herb, and spreads out ev'ry flow'r;

Annual for me, the grape, the rose renew

The juice nectareous, and the balmy dew. . .

For me, health gushes from a thousand springs;

Seas roll to waft me, suns to light me rise;

My foot-stool earth, my canopy the skies.

Alexander Pope (1688–1744)
English poet

WHAT'S THE BEST THING IN THE WORLD?
JUNE-ROSE BY MAY-DEW IMPEARLED . . .

ELIZABETH BARRETT BROWNING (1806–1861)
ENGLISH POET

Summer set lip to earth's bosom bare

And left the flushed print in a poppy there.

FRANCIS THOMPSON (1859–1907)
ENGLISH POET

*T*he exceeding beauty

of the earth

in her splendour yields

a new thought with

every

petal.

RICHARD JEFFERIES (1848–1887)
ENGLISH WRITER

What wondrous life is this I lead!

Ripe apples drop about my head;

The luscious clusters of the vine

Upon my mouth do crush their wine;

The nectarene, and curious peach,

Into my hands themselves do reach;

Stumbling on melons, as I pass,

Ensnared with flowers, I fall on grass.

Andrew Marvell (1621–1678)
English poet

IS NOT THE SECRET PURPOSE OF THIS SLY EARTH,
IN URGING A PAIR OF LOVERS, JUST TO MAKE
EVERYTHING LEAP WITH ECSTASY IN THEM?

Rainer Maria Rilke (1875–1926)
Czech-born German poet

Who has seen the wind?

Neither you nor I:

But when the trees bow down their heads,

The wind is passing by.

CHRISTINA ROSSETTI (1830–1894)
ENGLISH POET

The swallows are making them ready to fly,

Wheeling out on a windy sky:

Goodbye, Summer, good-bye, good-bye.

George Whyte-Melville (1821–1878)
Scottish poet

ALWAYS TOO SOON

THE TREES ARE STARTLED BY AUTUMN

Anonymous
14th-century Chinese poet

The
fall of
a leaf
is a
whisper
to the
living.

<small>DANISH PROVERB</small>

FOR ME WHO GO,

FOR YOU WHO STAY—

TWO AUTUMNS.

Taniguchi Buson (1716–1783)
Japanese painter and poet

Season of mists and mellow fruitfulness,

   Close bosom-friend of the maturing sun;

Conspiring with him how to load and bless

   With fruit the vines that round the thatch-eaves run;

To bend with apples the moss'd cottage-trees,

   And fill all fruit with ripeness to the core;

   To swell the gourd, and plump the hazel shells

With a sweet kernel; to set budding more,

And still more, later flowers for the bees,

Until they think warm days will never cease,

   For Summer has o'er-brimm'd their clammy cells.

JOHN KEATS (1795–1821)
ENGLISH POET

I AM THE LAST FLOWER OF AUTUMN.
I WAS ROCKED IN SUMMER'S CRADLE,
I WAS PUT ON WATCH AGAINST THE NORTH WIND,
RED FLAMES BURST OUT
ON MY WHITE CHEEK.
I AM THE LAST FLOWER OF THE AUTUMN.
I AM THE YOUNGEST SEED OF THE DEAD SPRING.

Edith Södergran (1892–1923)
Finnish writer

O

ut of the bosom of the air,

Out of the cloudfolds of her garment shaken,

Over the woodlands, brown and bare,

Over the harvest-fields forsaken,

Silent, and soft, and slow

Descends the snow.

HENRY WADSWORTH LONGFELLOW (1807–1882)
AMERICAN WRITER

I love snow, and all the forms

  Of the radiant frost;

I love waves, and winds, and storms,

  Everything almost

Which is Nature's, and may be

Untainted by man's misery.

Percy Bysshe Shelley (1792–1822)
English poet

Oh Winter, ruler of th' inverted year...

I crown thee king of intimate delights,

Fire-side enjoyments, home-born happiness,

And all the comforts that the lowly roof

Of undisturbed retirement and the hours

Of long uninterrupted evening know.

WILLIAM COWPER (1731–1800)
ENGLISH WRITER

Over the land freckled with snow half-thawed

The speculating rooks at their nests cawed

And saw from elm-tops, delicate as flower of grass,

What we below could not see, Winter pass.

EDWARD THOMAS (1878–1919)
ENGLISH POET AND CRITIC

. . . no more the frost

Candies the grass, or casts an icy cream

Upon the silver lake or crystal stream;

But the warm sun thaws the benumbed earth,

And makes it tender. . . .

Thomas Carew (1595–1639)
English poet

At Christmas I no more desire a rose

Than wish a snow in May's new-fangled mirth...

WILLIAM SHAKESPEARE (1564–1616)
ENGLISH DRAMATIST

There are seasons,
in human affairs,
of inward and
outward revolution,
when new depths
seem to be broken
up in the soul,
when new wants
are unfolded in
multitudes, and a
new and undefined
good is thirsted for.
There are periods
when...to dare, is
the highest wisdom.

WILLIAM ELLERY CHANNING
(1780–1842)
AMERICAN CLERGYMAN

One goes to Nature only for hints and half-truths. Her facts are crude until you have absorbed them or translated them. . . . It is not so much what we see as what the thing seen suggests.

JOHN BURROUGHS (1837–1921)
AMERICAN NATURALIST

NATURE NEVER WEARS A MEAN
APPEARANCE. NEITHER DOES THE
WISEST MAN EXTORT HER SECRET
AND LOSE HIS CURIOSITY BY
FINDING OUT ALL HER
PERFECTION.

Ralph Waldo Emerson (1803–1882)
American writer

However much
you knock at
nature's door,
she will never
answer you in
comprehensible
words.

IVAN TURGENEV (1818–1883)
RUSSIAN WRITER

FOUR SEASONS FILL THE MEASURE OF THE YEAR

THERE ARE FOUR SEASONS IN THE MIND OF MEN

JOHN KEATS (1795-182
ENGLISH POE

Therefore all seasons shall be sweet to thee,

Whether the summer clothe the general earth

With greenness, or redbreast sit and sing

Betwixt the tufts of snow on the bare branch

Of mossy apple-tree, while the nigh thatch

Smokes in the sun-thaw; whether the eve-drops fall

Heard only in the trances of the blast,

Or if the secret ministry of frost

Shall hang them up in silent icicles,

Quietly shining to the quiet moon.

SAMUEL TAYLOR COLERIDGE (1772–1834)
ENGLISH POET

ILLUSTRATION ACKNOWLEDGMENTS

COVER: *Gathering Primroses*, after Miles Birket Foster (Fine Art Photographic Library Limited)

pp. 2–3 [detail]: *The Bluebell Wood*, P. F. Robinet (Fine Art Photographic Library Limited)

p. 6 [detail]: *Still Life*, Jan van Os

p. 7 [detail]: *Winter Fruits and Flowers*, Jane Inglis (Fine Art Photographic Library Limited)

p. 8: *Picking Blackberries*, John Haskins (Daryl Davies (British Fine Art) Ringwood, Hampshire)

p. 9: *Figures on a Snowy Woodland Way*, Everadus Pegano Mirani (MacConnal-Mason Gallery, St. James's, London SW1)

p. 10: *Country Lane*, Hubert Squires

p. 13 [detail]: *Winter Sun, Westminster*, John Donaldson (The Omell Galleries, London & Windsor)

p. 14: *Bluebells*, Helen Allingham (Fine Art Photographic Library Limited)

p. 16–17: *Deer in a Snowy Wooded Landscape*, Arthur Julius Thiele (Bourne Gallery Reigate and Fine Art Photographic Library Limited)

p. 19: *Gathering Primroses*, after Miles Birket Foster (Fine Art Photographic Library Limited)

p. 20: *Spring Time*, Alfred East

p. 21 [detail]: *A Corner of a Summer Garden*, Harry E. James

p. 23: *Bullfinch*, Basil Ede

p. 24: *Crossing the Daisy Field*, Philip W. Holyoake (Fine Art Photographic Library Limited)

p. 26: *Earth*, Jan "Velvet" Brueghel

p. 28: *Picking Poppies*, Alfred Glendening

p. 29: *Summer Rhapsody*, Vernon Ward

p. 31 [detail]: *The Gardener's Shed*, from an original Baxter print

p. 33: *Summer Idleness*, Roger Joseph Jourdain (MacConnal-Mason Gallery, St. James's, London SW1)

p. 34: *Hertfordshire By-Way*, Hubert Squires

p. 36: *Les Glaneuse*, Leon L'Hermitte (MacConnal-Mason Gallery, St. James's, London SW1)

pp. 38–39: *Winter Dawn*, Hubert Squires

p. 40 [detail]: *Skating on the Ice*, Van Leverbroeck (Fine Art Photographic Library Limited)

p. 41 [detail]: *Low Tide, Blakeney Marshes, Norfolk*, Vernon Ward

p. 42: *Middeburgh, 17th Century*, Christoffel van den Berge

p. 44: *Evening Reflection—River Wye, Bakewell*, Rex Preston (Granby Gallery, Bakewell, Derbyshire)

p. 46: *A View of Snowdon*, Sidney Richard Percy